ORIENTAL PEARL

Simon Rose

www.av2books.com

MEDIA ENHANCED BOOKS
AV²
BY WEIGL™
ADDED VALUE • AUDIO VISUAL

AV² provides enriched content that supplements and complements this book. Weigl's AV² books strive to create inspired learning and engage young minds in a total learning experience.

Your AV² Media Enhanced books come alive with...

Audio
Listen to sections of the book read aloud.

Key Words
Study vocabulary, and complete a matching word activity.

Video
Watch informative video clips.

Quizzes
Test your knowledge.

Embedded Weblinks
Gain additional information for research.

Slide Show
View images and captions, and prepare a presentation.

Try This!
Complete activities and hands-on experiments.

... and much, much more!

Go to **www.av2books.com**, and enter this book's unique code.

BOOK CODE

T101299

AV² by Weigl brings you media enhanced books that support active learning.

Published by AV² by Weigl
350 5th Avenue, 59th Floor
New York, NY 10118
Websites: www.av2books.com   www.weigl.com

Library of Congress Control Number: 2013953159
ISBN 978-1-4896-0740-9 (hardcover)
ISBN 978-1-4896-0741-6 (softcover)
ISBN 978-1-4896-0742-3 (single user eBook)
ISBN 978-1-4896-0743-0 (multi-user eBook)

Printed in the United States of America in North Mankato, Minnesota
1 2 3 4 5 6 7 8 9 0 18 17 16 15 14

052014
WEP310514

Editor: Heather Kissock
Design: Terry Paulhus

Every reasonable effort has been made to trace ownership and to obtain permission to reprint copyright material. The publishers would be pleased to have any errors or omissions brought to their attention so that they may be corrected in subsequent printings.

Weigl acknowledges Getty Images, Alamy, Newscom, Landov, and Dreamstime as its primary image suppliers for this title.

Contents

What Is the Oriental Pearl?

The Oriental Pearl Tower rises high above the Chinese city of Shanghai. The communications tower is one of the city's main landmarks and a major tourist attraction. People visit the Oriental Pearl for the amazing views of the city it provides. The tower has more than 15 observation decks, each offering a different perspective on the city below.

When it was completed in 1994, the Oriental Pearl was the tallest structure in China. It remained so until 2007, when it was surpassed by the Shanghai World Financial Center. However, at 1,535 feet (468 meters) tall, the Oriental Pearl is still one of the tallest television towers in the world.

Besides offering a breathtaking view, the Oriental Pearl is also part of the city's cultural core. It stands in the center of a complex containing entertainment venues, restaurants, shopping, and a cruise dock. The tower's observation levels feature unique cultural experiences. At different levels, visitors can find the Shanghai History Museum, the Space Hotel, and a revolving restaurant.

The Oriental Pearl has been lauded as one of the top 10 views in Shanghai by visitors and residents alike.

Snapshot of China

Located in eastern Asia, China is one of the world's largest countries by area. To its north lie Russia and Mongolia. Kazakhstan, Kyrgyzstan, Tajikistan, Afghanistan, and Pakistan share China's western border. China is bordered by India, Nepal, Bhutan, Myanmar, Laos, and Vietnam to its south. North Korea sits to its east. The Yellow Sea, East China Sea, and South China Sea also form part of China's eastern border.

INTRODUCING CHINA

CAPITAL CITY: Beijing

FLAG:

POPULATION: 1.36 billion (2013)

OFFICIAL LANGUAGE: Mandarin

CURRENCY: Yuan (Renminbi)

CLIMATE: Mainly temperate, with temperature extremes in the north and south

SUMMER TEMPERATURE: Average of 72° Fahrenheit (22° Celsius)

WINTER TEMPERATURE: Average of 50° F (10° C)

TIME ZONE: China Standard Time (CST)

China
- - - - International Boundary
★ National Capital

0   500 miles
0   500 kilometers

Chinese Words to Know

When visiting a foreign country, it is always a good idea to know some words and phrases in the local language. Practice the phrases below to prepare for a trip to China.

qing wen
Excuse me

nihao
Hello

xiexie
Thank you

ni hui shuo yingyu ma?
Do you speak English?

shi
Yes

duoshao qian?
How much does it cost?

bu yong xie
You are welcome.

duibuqi
Sorry

zai jian
Goodbye

bu shi
No

nihao ma?
How are you?

ni jiao shenma mingzi?
What is your name?

A Step Back in Time

In 1993, the government of China established a **special economic zone** in Shanghai called the Pudong New Area. Part of the Pudong district was called the Lujiazui Finance and Trade Zone. This area was to become China's new financial center. Shortly after the zone was established, city planners began working to build up the area so that it would attract new businesses. One of the first structures to begin construction was the Oriental Pearl. Although it was to serve an important function as a communications tower, the Oriental Pearl's futuristic design was intended to transform the skyline of Shanghai and become a new symbol of the city.

CONSTRUCTION TIMELINE

1990
The Chinese government announces plans to develop a special economic zone in Shanghai. It is to be called the Pudong New Area.

1990
The state government approves the creation of the Lujiazui Finance and Trade Zone in the newly announced Pudong New Area.

1990
Construction of the Oriental Pearl begins as part of an effort to improve the image of the Pudong area.

1994
Construction of the Oriental Pearl is completed on October 1.

1995
Nine television stations and ten radio stations begin broadcasting from the Oriental Pearl's antenna.

Pudong is named for its location. Dong means "east" in Chinese, and Pudong is situated on the east side of the Huangpu River.

Several other structures soon followed. Construction of the Jin Mao Tower was completed in 1999, becoming China's tallest building. It lost this title eight years later when its neighbor, the Shanghai World Financial Center skyscraper, completed construction. As one of China's leading business hubs, the Lujiazui area continues to develop, and several new buildings are currently under construction.

The Jin Mao Tower and Shanghai World Financial Center stand adjacent to each other in the center of the Lujiazui Finance and Trade Zone.

2001
The exhibition room of the Shanghai History Museum opens at the base of the tower.

2009
The Skydeck observation platform, made entirely of glass, is opened.

2010
The tower's antenna catches fire on April 13, but the blaze is quickly put out by firefighters.

2013
In August, the exterior of the tower is cleaned for the first time since it was constructed.

2013
In September, officials announce that the Oriental Pearl will undergo an extensive renovation that is expected to take seven months.

The Oriental Pearl antenna fire happened in the early morning hours after lightning had been spotted in the area.

One month after cleaning the Oriental Pearl's exterior, it was announced that work would commence to fix cracks in the structure.

The Oriental Pearl's Location

The Oriental Pearl is located in a key tourist area, where past and present stand opposite each other. As part of the Lujiazui Finance and Trade Zone, the tower is located on the east bank of the Huangpu River. Lujiazui represents modern Shanghai and has many tall, contemporary buildings. Images of the Lujiazui skyline are frequently used to promote tourism and business in Shanghai. Hundreds of corporations, both from China and other countries, are based in the area. There are also many hotels catering to tourists and business travelers.

On the opposite side of the river to Lujiazui is a historic district of Shanghai known as the Bund. This is the old financial and business area of the city and has impressive buildings in many different **architectural** styles. The Bund is located on the waterfront in central Shanghai and was once the center of the Shanghai International Settlement. This was where banks and businesses from the United States, Great Britain, and many European countries had their bases for trading with China in the 19th and early 20th centuries. With its many historical buildings, the Bund is one of Shanghai's main tourist destinations.

The Oriental Pearl is situated on a peninsula formed by a bend in the Huangpu River.

The Oriental Pearl Today

The Oriental Pearl is one of Shanghai's most distinctive landmarks. The tower is a symbol not only of Shanghai, but of modern China's rapid **commercial** expansion in recent decades. In 2007, the Chinese National Tourism Administration awarded the tower a "AAAAA" ranking, noting it as one of the country's most important tourist attractions. It is estimated that approximately three million people visit the Oriental Pearl each year.

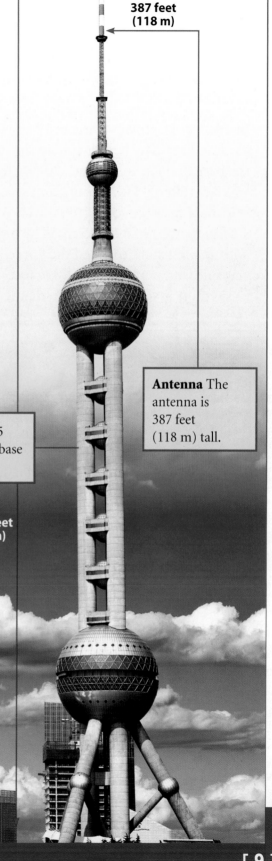

387 feet (118 m)

Antenna The antenna is 387 feet (118 m) tall.

Height The tower is 1,535 feet (468 m) tall from the base to the top of the antenna.

1,535 feet (468 m)

Weight The estimated weight of the tower is 120,000 tons (108,862 metric tons).

Outside the Oriental Pearl

The Oriental Pearl has a distinctive design that makes the structure instantly recognizable on the modern Shanghai skyline.

Spheres The tower features 11 spheres of varying sizes. The largest sphere sits near the base of the tower. It has a diameter of 164 feet (50 m). The second largest sphere is located near the top of the tower. It has a diameter of 148 feet (45 m). The highest and smallest sphere, called the Space Capsule, sits at a height of 1,099 feet (335 m). It is 46 feet (14 m) in diameter.

The Oriental Pearl's large lower sphere houses the world's highest indoor roller coaster.

The Oriental Pearl's stanchions and columns act as the structure's legs, providing support for the rest of the tower.

Stanchions and Columns Three large slanted **stanchions** support the Oriental Pearl Tower and hold it in position. Each stanchion is about 23 feet (7 m) wide and extends deep underground. Three columns, each about 30 feet (9 m) in diameter, stand in the center of the tower between the two largest spheres. These columns also link several of the smaller spheres to each other.

Antenna The Oriental Pearl is primarily a communications tower. The antenna at the top of the tower sends and receives local television and radio signals. The 387-foot (118-m) tall antenna serves the Shanghai area with approximately 30 channels for both television and radio broadcasts.

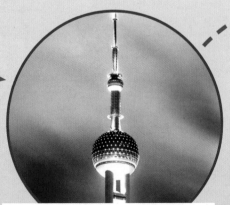

The added height of the antenna has helped to make the Oriental Pearl the second-tallest TV tower in China and the fourth tallest TV tower in the world.

Cruise Dock The Oriental Pearl Cruise Dock is found a few steps away from the tower on the bank of the Huangpu River. From here, visitors to the Oriental Pearl can take a 40-minute boat cruise to view the sights of Pudong and the Bund before returning to the tower.

The Oriental Pearl Cruise Dock is designed to resemble a seagull spreading its wings as it appears to fly.

One of the best views of the Oriental Pearl's evening lights is from across the river in the Bund.

Lights At night, the Oriental Pearl's super-bright LED lights glisten in the night sky, its many colors adding a festive look to the Shanghai skyline. Computer systems adjust the lighting in accordance with the weather conditions. The tower is sometimes lit in particular colors for special events. For example, the tower was illuminated with pink lights to celebrate International Women's Day in 2012.

VIRTUAL TOUR

The Oriental Pearl is open daily from 8:00 a.m. to 9:30 p.m. Admission prices depend on the level guests intend to visit.

Inside the Oriental Pearl

The Oriental Pearl has many features that provide a truly unique visitor experience. People can experience various forms of entertainment as well as learn about the city of Shanghai. Many of the Oriental Pearl's attractions pay tribute to the tower's space-like appearance.

Observation Levels The Oriental Pearl's observation levels allow visitors to view the surrounding city from different heights. The highest observation deck is found in the Space Capsule, at a height of 1,122 feet (342 m). The Sightseeing Galleria is 863 feet (263 m) above the ground and is located in the tower's second largest sphere. The tower's lowest observation level is called Game City and is located in the largest sphere at a height of 322 feet (98 m). This level also has an outside viewing area.

The Transparent Observatory is located in the second sphere. Here, visitors can experience a panoramic view of Shanghai and the Huangpu River through the transparent glass under their feet.

The Oriental Pearl's futuristic appearance and space themes make it an ideal location for space-related events. In 2012, a new *Star Wars* video game was promoted at the tower.

Science Fantasy World The Oriental Pearl Science Fantasy World is located in the tower's lowest sphere. This venue has several attractions that allow visitors to experience different environments. Attractions such as Journey Through the Forest, Trip to the South Pole, and Hot Air Balloon provide visitors with unique adventures in the tower.

Shanghai History Museum The Shanghai History Museum is located at the base of the tower. The museum takes people on a journey through approximately 100 years of the city's history, from about 1843 to 1949. It explores Shanghai's role as a port city and the influence of foreign settlers on the city. The history of Shanghai comes to life through displays of historical artifacts, documents, and pictures, as well as special audio-visual presentations.

Many of the museum's exhibits demonstrate aspects of daily life in old Shanghai.

Each of the hotel's spheres contains two levels and four rooms.

Hotel and Entertainment

The 20-room Space Hotel is located in the five spheres situated between the two largest spheres. The Oriental Pearl also has a number of entertainment and dining facilities located in the two upper spheres. People visiting the tower can demonstrate their musical talent in the tower's karaoke rooms or go dancing at the Oriental Pearl disco. Coffee bars, restaurants, and gift shops are also found throughout the tower levels.

Revolving Restaurant The tower's revolving restaurant is located at 876 feet (267 m) and rotates fully once every two hours. The restaurant offers spectacular views of Shanghai and the surrounding area. It is the second highest revolving restaurant in Asia and can accommodate up to 350 people.

Visitors can experience a 360-degree view of Shanghai when dining at the Revolving Restaurant.

Big Ideas behind the Oriental Pearl

The designers of the Oriental Pearl wanted to build one of the world's tallest structures to stand as a symbol of modern Shanghai and attract visitors from all over the world. They wanted it to pay tribute to Chinese culture, while also having commercial appeal. As with all buildings, safety was also a significant factor in selecting the materials used to build the Oriental Pearl.

The pipa dates back to the 2nd century AD. It is commonly heard in Chinese opera, but can also be played as a solo instrument.

Poetry and the Pearl

The design of the Oriental Pearl is said to be based on a poem by Bai Juyi. He was a Chinese poet who lived in the late eighth and early ninth centuries. His poem *Pipa Song* was inspired by the sprinkling sound made by a pipa, or Chinese lute. Music from the pipa is described in the poem as sounding like various sizes of pearls gently falling onto a jade plate. The tower's spheres were designed to represent the pearls, and the grassy area at the base of the tower symbolizes the jade plate.

The Glass Floor

The Transparent Observatory has a 7,535 square foot (700 square m) glass floor. Due to the number of visitors this level was expected to receive, it was important for the floor to be specially reinforced. The observatory's flooring is made with **laminated glass** containing an **interlayer** called SentryGlas®. Laminated glass is designed to hold together even when shattered. SentryGlas® is 100 times stiffer and five times stronger than standard laminated glass interlayers. It is designed to withstand high stress **loads** and is ideal for use in glass flooring.

The SentryGlas® interlayer is very clear, so it works well in locations such as the Oriental Pearl, where visitors like to take photographs through glass.

Science at Work in the Oriental Pearl

Many people were involved in the construction of the Oriental Pearl. Up to 2,000 people worked on the site at any one time during the building process. Cranes and other machines were also needed to complete such a tall structure. Materials used in the construction of the tower include steel and reinforced concrete.

Reinforced concrete uses hidden metal bars to help it withstand the forces of compression, or squeezing, and tension, or pulling.

Concrete and Steel

Concrete and steel were the key materials used in the tower's construction. Concrete is a very strong material that is able to withstand many different environmental conditions. It is highly resistant to freezing and thawing, is resistant to wear, and is watertight. Much of the tower's concrete is reinforced. Reinforced concrete has metal bars inside it. To make reinforced concrete, steel bars are placed inside a mold, and concrete is added. When the concrete sets inside the mold, the bars bond to it. This strengthens the concrete.

Tower Cranes

One of the main challenges in building a tall structure is getting the materials up to the higher levels. Tower cranes are often seen at construction sites. These cranes are hundreds of feet (m) tall, and the horizontal **jib** that does the lifting can reach out almost as far. The crane's base is bolted to a large concrete pad to prevent the crane from falling over. The base connects to the mast, or tower. At the top of the mast is the slewing unit. This contains the gears and motor that allow the crane to rotate. The long jib on top of this unit carries the materials being moved. They are moved along the jib by a trolley.

The maximum load that a typical tower crane can lift is 39,683 pounds (18 metric tons).

VIRTUAL TOUR

The Oriental Pearl cost more than $100 million U.S. to build.

The Oriental Pearl's Builders

Designing and building the Oriental Pearl required a team of construction professionals. The designers and **engineers** relied on the skills of high riggers, crane operators, concrete finishers, and people from many other trades to complete the project.

Tsinghua University is located in the Chinese capital city of Beijing. It is one of the country's best-known universities. More than 25,000 students attend the school every year to study subjects ranging from philosophy to engineering.

Jiang Huan Cheng

Chief Designer

Jiang Huan Cheng was the designer in charge of planning the Oriental Pearl. Born in 1938, Cheng went to Tsinghua University following his high school graduation. His main course of study was **civil engineering**. He graduated with his degree in 1963. In 1980, Cheng was granted permission to work for a design firm in the United Kingdom. It was here that he had the opportunity to work on several international projects and advance his design skills. Upon his return to China, he went to work for the Shanghai Institute of Architectural Design and Research, one of China's most prestigious architectural firms. By 1989, he was the chief director of the company's design team. When the competition to design a tower in Shanghai was announced, Cheng and his team came up with more than 30 concepts. They submitted five to the competition, and the Oriental Pearl concept won.

East China Architectural Design and Research Institute

Engineers

Engineering work for the tower was completed by the East China Architectural Design and Research Institute (ECADI). Founded in the 1950s, ECADI is now one of China's leading architectural design companies and has completed more than 10,000 projects in China and around the world. Besides the Oriental Pearl, some of its best-known projects include the Shanghai World Financial Center and the Jin Mao Tower.

One of the East China Architectural Design and Research Institute's more recent projects was Shanghai's Performing Arts Center. Built for the 2010 World Expo, the building houses theaters, music clubs, and art galleries.

Concrete Finishers

Concrete finishers are construction workers that specialize in building with concrete. They work on both indoor and outdoor projects. Concrete finishers pour wet concrete into casts, or molds, and spread it to a desired thickness, depending on the project. They level and smooth the surfaces and edges of the concrete. Concrete finishers also repair, waterproof, and restore existing concrete surfaces. At the Oriental Pearl, concrete finishers worked on floors, walls, and columns throughout the structure.

Concrete finishing is very physical work. It involves lifting, bending, kneeling, and carrying heavy bags of cement.

Crane Operators

Tower crane operators are responsible for lifting and moving building materials, machinery, and heavy objects on construction sites. They often work at great heights and need special training for their job. Tower crane operators communicate with workers on the ground or inside the building with hand signals or by radio. They use equipment in their **cab** to move the crane around and to monitor the progress of the job.

To perform their job well, tower crane operators need to have good balance, coordination, and the ability to judge distances.

High Riggers

High riggers are construction workers who work at extreme heights. They install equipment such as cables, ropes, pulleys, and **winches** to safely move or position different types of machinery and construction materials. They also decide which equipment will be strong enough or best suited for a particular project. High riggers often work closely with crane operators. They help direct the crane when it is moving materials or equipment.

Although they wear safety harnesses, high riggers have one of the most dangerous jobs in the construction industry.

Similar Structures around the World

Towers similar to the Oriental Pearl can be found in various parts of the world. Like the Oriental Pearl, many of these towers were built as communications facilities. Most, however, are better known as tourist attractions that bring in millions of visitors every year.

Tokyo Skytree

BUILT: 2012
LOCATION: Tokyo, Japan
DESIGN: Nikken Sekkei
DESCRIPTION: The Tokyo Skytree is the tallest **freestanding** structure in Japan. Acting as both a broadcasting and observation tower, Skytree is at the center of one of Tokyo's newest commercial development projects. At 2,080 feet (634 m), it is currently the world's tallest tower and is also the world's tallest structure built on an island.

The CN Tower's LED lights illuminate the structure each night from dusk to 2:00 am.

The Tokyo Skytree was designed to withstand high winds and earthquakes.

CN Tower

BUILT: 1976
LOCATION: Toronto, Canada
DESIGN: John Andrews, WZMH Architects
DESCRIPTION: The CN Tower is an observation and communications tower that is 1,815.5 feet (553.3 m) tall. The tower was both the tallest tower and the tallest freestanding structure in the world for 34 years. Today, it remains the tallest freestanding structure in the Western Hemisphere. The CN Tower is one of the most recognizable symbols of Canada and holds a distinctive place in Toronto's skyline. It is a major Canadian tourist attraction, receiving approximately 1.5 million visitors every year.

Ostankino Tower

BUILT: 1967
LOCATION: Moscow, Russia
DESIGN: Nikolai Nikitin
DESCRIPTION: Ostankino Tower is a freestanding radio and television tower located in the Ostankino district of Moscow. It was built to commemorate the 50th anniversary of Russia's **October Revolution**. The tower is 1,772 feet (539.5 m) tall and has been the tallest freestanding structure in Europe for 42 years. It is currently the fourth tallest tower in the world.

In August 2000, fire broke out in the Ostankino Tower, causing serious damage to the structure. Repairs and upgrades were complete by 2004.

Milad Tower

BUILT: 2008
LOCATION: Tehran, Iran
DESIGN: Dr. Mohammad Reza Hafezi
DESCRIPTION: Milad Tower, also known as Borj-e Milad, is a telecommunications and observation tower. It is part of Tehran's International Trade and Convention Center. At 1,427 feet (435 m), Milad Tower is the sixth tallest tower in the world. The pod at the top of the tower has 12 floors and contains restaurants, observation decks, and a public art gallery.

Milad Tower's shaft is octagonal in shape, a tribute to Iran's Persian heritage. Octagons are a common feature in traditional Persian architecture.

Issues Facing the Oriental Pearl

A great deal of planning went into the building of the Oriental Pearl. While designing the building, planners had to consider issues related to its height. They also had to consider the safety of people inside the tower and the surrounding area.

WHAT IS THE ISSUE?

Due to its height, the Oriental Pearl is subject to extremely high winds.	The height of the tower makes fighting a fire very difficult, especially on the upper levels.	The Shanghai area has had earthquakes in the past measuring between 5 and 6 on the **Richter scale**.

EFFECTS

The tower could sway too far in high winds and be so badly damaged that it could collapse.	Since elevators are unsafe to use if a fire breaks out, people would be stranded on the higher levels.	The Oriental Pearl Tower could be seriously damaged in the event of an earthquake.

ACTION TAKEN

The tower is built to withstand winds of up to 373 miles (600 kilometers) per hour. The antenna can also sway 5 feet (1.5 m) from the core without being damaged.	Fireproof materials were used to build the tower, and the city's fire department is well equipped to deal with any fires that may occur. When the antenna caught fire in 2010, the fire was put out by firefighters in about an hour.	The tower's **foundation** extends 59 feet (18 m) underground. This makes the structure very stable and provides resistance to the damaging effects of earthquakes.

Build a Crane

Cranes do much of the heavy lifting in construction projects. To do the work required of them, these complex machines are made up of several smaller simple machines. A pulley is used to lift materials to where they are needed. A lever provides support to the pulley. A wheel and axle secures the cable that runs through the pulley.

To see these three simple machines at work, build your own crane by following these instructions.

Materials
- Ruler
- Pencil
- String
- Metal hook or magnet
- Paper clips

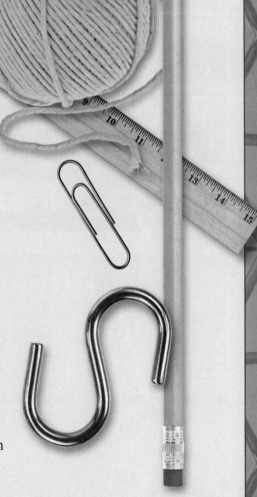

Instructions
1. Wrap one end of the string around the pencil.

2. Tie the hook or magnet to the other end of the string.

3. Hold the pencil against the ruler, and drape the end holding the magnet or hook over the edge of the ruler. If the ruler has openings in it, thread the string through one of the holes.

4. Hold the ruler over the paper clips, and try to pick them up with the hook or magnet. When you have connected the magnet and paper clips, begin lifting the paper clip by rolling more string onto the pencil.

5. Observe the role each part of your crane plays in the lifting process. Which piece of your crane is the wheel and axle? Which is the lever? Does your crane have a pulley?

The Oriental Pearl Quiz

Q How tall is the Oriental Pearl Tower?

A 1,535 feet (468 m)

Q How many spheres does the tower have?

A 11

Q Who designed the Oriental Pearl Tower?

A Jiang Huan Cheng

Q Where is the highest observation level in the tower?

A The Space Capsule

Key Words

architectural: relating to the design of buildings

cab: the covered compartment of a heavy vehicle or machine in which the driver or operator sits

civil engineering: the branch of engineering concerned with the design of public works, including buildings and other structures

commercial: concerned with earning money

engineers: people who apply scientific principles to the design of structures

foundation: construction below the ground that distributes the load of a building or other structure built on top of it

freestanding: not supported by another structure

interlayer: a layer placed between other layers

jib: the long arm of a mechanical crane

laminated glass: glass made with plates of plastic, resin, or other materials to prevent shattering

loads: weights or sources of pressure carried by an object

October Revolution: an uprising that occurred in Russia in 1917 that led to the toppling of the Russian monarchy

Richter scale: a scale that measures the strength of an earthquake

special economic zone: a region set up by a government to facilitate trade and commerce with other countries

stanchions: long beams or posts used to support a building

winches: lifting devices made up of ropes or chains running around a rotating drum

Index

Log on to www.av2books.com

AV² by Weigl brings you media enhanced books that support active learning. Go to www.av2books.com, and enter the special code found on page 2 of this book. You will gain access to enriched and enhanced content that supplements and complements this book. Content includes video, audio, weblinks, quizzes, a slide show, and activities.

AV² Online Navigation

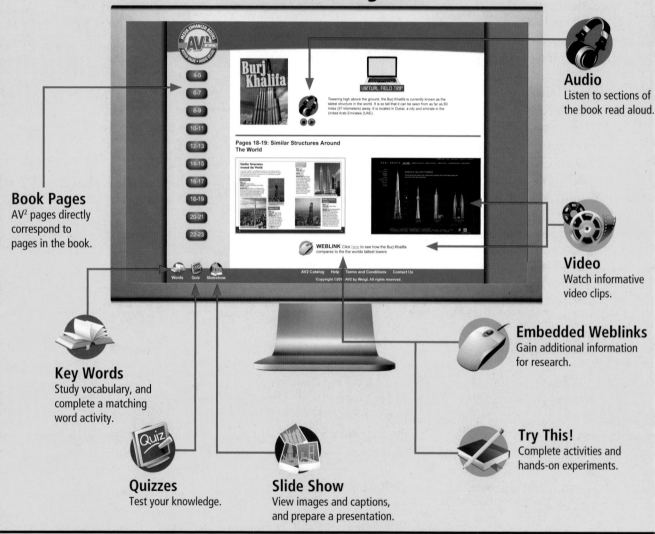

Audio
Listen to sections of the book read aloud.

Book Pages
AV² pages directly correspond to pages in the book.

Video
Watch informative video clips.

Key Words
Study vocabulary, and complete a matching word activity.

Embedded Weblinks
Gain additional information for research.

Quizzes
Test your knowledge.

Slide Show
View images and captions, and prepare a presentation.

Try This!
Complete activities and hands-on experiments.

AV² was built to bridge the gap between print and digital. We encourage you to tell us what you like and what you want to see in the future.

Sign up to be an AV² Ambassador at www.av2books.com/ambassador.